THE NEW WORLD ORDER AND THE DESTRUCTION OF AMERICA

Major (Ret.) James F. Linzey

LINZEY PUBLISHING HOUSE

THE NEW WORLD ORDER
AND THE DESTRUCTION OF AMERICA
Major (Ret.) James F. Linzey

Cover Design by Istvan Szabo, Ifj.
http://www.sapphireguardian.com

Printed in the United States of America
ISBN 978-1-936857-21-0

Linzey Publishing House
P.O. Box 300366
Escondido, California

OTHER BOOKS BY JAMES F. LINZEY

A Divine Appointment in Washington, DC
Baptism in the Spirit
The Holy Spirit
Moral Leadership
Why the Conservative Mind Matters
(Contributing author)

PREFACE

In November 1985, I was given a direct commission into the United States Air Force Reserves as a chaplain with the rank of first lieutenant. At the same time I was a schoolteacher in the Los Angeles Unified School District. I was in Watts not far from the horrifying beating of Reginald Denny, which was the beginning of severe rioting and looting. I was, in fact, driving out of Watts as that occurred, as quickly as I was allowed to drive by law, on my way to an event I had planned at Norton AFB in San Bernardino, California.

For several years up to that time, I had a surreal feeling that what I saw in society was not as it seemed to be. I could not pinpoint what I sensed, but it seemed like there was a subversive spirit undermining American society. Yet I could not substantiate it. No one told me this. I did not know what to do with what I sensed. So I began asking questions in the military to individuals only if I learned that they knew something I did not know, and if I felt safe to ask. Much to my amazement, I began learning things I did not know, which substantiated my discernment that something was dreadfully wrong in America.

The Dream

In January of 1987, I dreamed that I was in a concentration camp for Christians. I was in an area fenced in with a chain link fence that had barbed wire on top. The area seemed rectangular, front to back. Other Christians were in there with me. I don't know how many were there, but I remember seeing about a dozen or more people. We could not see the sky. For some reason it was not visible inside the compound. Perhaps the lack of a sky symbolized darkness. In front were some American soldiers. Suddenly they began mowing us down with automatic weapons. I found myself grabbing for metal folding chairs I had not previously seen, and, with others, I began shielding myself from the bullets. After a while it stopped.

From out of nowhere, Christians rushed to the front left corner of the compound in a panic and tried to climb over the fence. They failed to get over. Then they rushed to the front right corner and succeeded at getting over to escape the hellish nightmare. I joined them as fast as I could. As soon as I climbed over into freedom, I could see the clear blue sky.

Just then, as quick as we were free, I saw in the sky that they were coming for us. Helicopters were flying our way. We looked for a place to hide, but there was no place to go. The only object near us was a set of bleachers. And that was no place to hide, though some tried. We were again about to be arrested. Suddenly I woke up, startled.

Since then, I've had three more dreams similar to this one. The two following dreams were also in 1987. The fourth dream was in 2010.

The Role of America

Historically, the role of any nation's Armed Forces has been to secure its nation's borders, shores and airspace. But the United States is failing on all three fronts.

Historically, the role of any nation's government has been to establish and adhere to sound monetary policies. But the United States is spending itself purposely into oblivion, and it is being "told" what its policies will be and that she must adhere to them.

And, historically, the role of peace-loving nations has been to respect the sovereignty of all other nations and to attend to their own internal affairs. But the United States is too involved in the affairs of other nations, and it has allowed other nations to become too involved in the inner workings of the United States.

The contents of this book was originally prepared as a speech, prepared by my former college English professor who assisted me in the research and the writing. I am not an expert in the subject matter, but I sensed a "Call to Duty" to come to my country's aid to do my part to save her as any respectable human being would do, and as every minister of the Gospel is called to do, and to prevent what I saw in dreams from becoming a reality.

DEDICATION

To All the nations of the world which have already lost their God-given freedoms thanks to the New World Order and free nations who did nothing to stop it, and whose turn it is to lose their freedoms if they do not wake up

CONTENTS

INTRODUCTION

From our first sense of our parents, we are learning the way that life is to be. Our parents begin programming us according to their own worldviews. Our parents' views of the world were determined by their parents, along with the media, their own education and the rest of their environment. Formal education adds to our worldview, because it is often a kind of indoctrination where the proper views are taught. Alternative views of things and the rejection of established ideas are discouraged.

As we grow up, our entire understanding of the world and current affairs is filtered through the mass media, and then interpreted by journalists and experts. Can you remember ever seeing a major event on TV without someone commenting and interpreting it afterward? The views of these supposed experts become our views simply because we are not offered any alternatives. We give our decision-making abilities to these few people in charge of our world, and these people are increasingly far from us, moving from local council power, to county, state and federal powers.

Regulation

The society around us determines our experience of life. The basic premise is that each individual should be a minute part of the global machine of consumerism led by Western multinational corporations and banks. Every other consideration is subordinate to the prime motivation of profit. Those in positions of influence—politicians, bankers, corporate executives and media moguls—have been successful with the profit system, so they have an interest in maintaining the status quo and passing it along. This idea of consumerism shapes all aspects of our lives through education, the media, health care, cultural and sporting events, and even religion. The regulation of life has begun taking place.

With these framing conditions, the system regulates itself: Individuals with attitudes that suit the perpetuation of the system achieve status and influence. The same attitudes control education, governments and banks and therefore exert an influence over every part of our thoughts and opinions. Individuals with attitudes contrary to the furthering of the system are looked upon with disfavor—in fact, they are usually not chosen for positions of advancement in the big corporations. Being in favor with big corporations results in power, wealth and progressive success.

Power, wealth and information come from many sources, but basically they have been gained and maintained via warfare, exploitation and control of the world's economic systems. With the acceleration in technological development, those in power have tried to realize their ambitions more swiftly, and they have usually been able to do so. Because a few have power over the many, opportunity arises to control or manipulate the many that are subservient. As long as there are submitted people who want or need more, the powerful people will be able to make use of them for profit.

Historical Views: *Accidental* and *Conspiracy*

William Blasé points out that there are two basic views of history. One we call the **"Accidental View."** This is the view the majority of people accept. It is the notion that events in history basically occur by accident and are the result of the conditions existing at the time. Events just occur, and there is no real meaning to them or connection between them. This is the view accepted by the news media.

The second view is called the **"Conspiracy View."** This is the cause and effect view, which holds that major events in history are the result of careful planning by the powerful few. All major events in the world are carried out with a desired goal in mind. This view of history is ridiculed, and its proponents are called delusional, William Blasé says, because those who want to debunk it have no real evidence for debunking it (Blasé, 2). Therefore, the debunkers resort to calling names, trying to discredit those who do believe in a conspiracy theory.

Those who try to debunk the conspiracy view usually attack the person who holds the view rather than the view itself. An example would be the militia movement in the United States. State militias have been forming all across the nation. The militia movement claims that the government is becoming socialistic and that the freedoms of the American people are in danger. The militia movements also speak of the loss of United States sovereignty to the United Nations. Many claim that all of this connection to the United Nations is an intentional plan to bring about a world government. The mass media and the government have labeled these state militias as domestic terrorists, extremists and a general threat to freedom. The militia groups' views are never discussed in detail, but the members of the militia are discredited by name-calling (Blasé, 4).

A regulated state militia is protected by the United States Constitution. A state militia is legal. Why are these militias forming? Are any of the claims of the militia movement actually true? Is the United States heading into a world government where rights are not protected? How far does the power of the few extend?

CHAPTER 1:
DESIRE AND NEED FOR POWER

The Purpose of Power

According to Fraser and Beeston, the goal of the power leaders, whom they call the "power elite," has been the creation of a system of world government, a world currency and bank, a world army, the control of public opinion culminating in a micro-chipped population connected to a central computer, and the destruction of any alternatives to the system. This plan has become popularly known as the New World Order.

Most people who help create this New World Order do so unknowingly.

The main manipulating groups are these (Fraser and Beeston):

1. Secret societies, such as Freemasonry, the Grand Orient Lodges, the Knights of Malta, the Black Nobility and the Brotherhood.

2. The Royal Institute of International Affairs (RIA), based at Chatham House in London and formed in 1920 by the Anglo/American delegations from the Treaty of Versailles meetings. The RIA is a think tank, but it also determines British policy. Funding is derived from its corporate members, a list of government departments, petrochemical companies, merchant and high street banks, newspapers, television stations, the Church of England and Amnesty International.

3. The Council on Foreign Relations (CFR), the American wing of the RIA, is composed of anyone who has influence in American or global politics.
4. The Bilderberg Group (BIL), convened in 1954 by Polish socialist Joseph Retinger, a major voice behind the European Union. It was to be a group of leading politicians and their advisors, executives from media, banking and multinational corporations, educators and military leaders who would meet to discuss the global future by addressing matters of critical importance in an off-the-record manner.

The Power of Conspiracy

William Blasé believes there is a drive (or conspiracy) by the powerful world elite, who are working to instill a One World totalitarian socialist government. He claims to have cross-checked and confirmed the accuracy of every one of his sources and statements. However, he does not give those sources for his reader to also check out. So, though some of his ideas are interesting, they are not open to confirmation for accuracy. Blasé points out that the vast majority of people in the world do not believe in conspiracies. A dictionary defines *conspiracy* as the act of two or more people coming together to plot to do something that is illegal (Blasé, 1). The world is full of conspiracy. People conspire with work associates to get a better position over someone else. The politicians conspire to win public favor and votes. So, as far as the examples go, Blasé is absolutely correct. However, in defining the word *conspiracy* according to the examples he gives, he is changing the definition so that it is no longer the same as the one he gave from the dictionary. The key word in the dictionary definition is "illegal." There is nothing necessarily illegal in trying to get a better position or to gain votes. Therefore, we see he is using the word loosely—as an act of minor plotting or planning to gain an end that would benefit those who are doing the planning. Such actions can sometimes be illegal, but many times they are not. That means that those actions are not a conspiracy unless they are illegal.

Because so many people do not believe there is such a thing as a conspiracy, if the Power Elite do try to take over the government and economic systems, they will do so without full public acknowledgement.

The main thing every man fears is the unknown. When we are fearful, we may even willingly relinquish individual rights for the guarantee of our well-being being guaranteed to us (Henry Kissinger, an address to the Bilderbergers Group. May 21, 1992. Evian, France).

CHAPTER 2:
NEW WORLD ORDER

"New World Order" is a term used to describe the uniting of the world's superpowers to secure and maintain "global peace." It is true that world leaders are excited at the prospects for peace, and there has been much talk about entering a "new era" and about the establishment of a "New World Order" (Fraser and Beeston, 28). However, though such a "new" kind of "peace" may sound wonderful, we need to consider just how acceptable such a change is, and how much that peace may cost Americans.

The scheme to establish a New World Order appears in the United Nations documents, and also the treaties, which, once ratified by individual nations, become international law. The United Nations created the Commission for Global Governance. The Commission for Global Governance released a report entitled *Our Global Neighborhood*, which outlines a world court, a global tax and a global police force. Also, the U.S. State Department Publication 7277 outlines a one-world police force under the United Nations (Blasé, 12).

The coming one world government is being set up through three primary areas (Blasé, 13):

A. The Political Sphere—The published goal of the Council of Foreign Relations is a one-world government.

B. The Economic Sphere—the influence of free trade agreements and organizations, such as the International Monetary Fund, the World Bank and the Bank of International Settlements. The coming global monetary crisis will be used to institute a one-world currency that will be a debt-based currency. The technology has already been developed to issue biometric identification cards to individuals to be followed up with an implantable biochip.

C. The Religious Sphere—the World Council of Churches and the Parliament of World Religions are set up with a pantheistic/humanist philosophy.

In all of these spheres, the individual is subservient to the state.

CHAPTER 3:
CONTROL

The New World Order will try to control all of the essential parts and areas of the individual's life.

Economic Control

Moves toward the New World Order have been furthered by the development of the current banking and economic systems. Those who own the money in the world control the world. Let's look at the various ways money and economics influence the New World Order.

Interest and Banking.

Charging interest inflates the prices of goods since a large percentage of an item's cost is servicing the debts of the suppliers and manufacturers. The greater the debt, the higher the price. Banks use this high rate of inflation to justify raising interest rates in order to discourage borrowing. Economic depressions and booms are easily created by the banking institutions as they are controlling the amount of money and credit in circulation (Fraser and Beeston).

Banks extend their influence by manipulating the stock markets to gain controlling interests in multinational companies. For example, a bank refuses a loan to a company seeking expansion. As the value of the shares fall, the bank buys them before changing its mind and granting the loan. For a nation to prosper on a global economic basis, it must borrow from private moneylenders, and it borrows other people's money that does not exist in real terms. At the same time, people are borrowing from the same banks to pay their taxes and their mortgages. This means the banks can never lose. All wealth in circulation around the world belongs to them, or is owed to them, or will be dragged into their vaults via the banking system (Fraser and Beeston). The borrower is always a slave to the lender.

Small Businesses

Little by little the small businesses and companies are being destroyed and replaced by mega-businesses. The mom-and-pop stores have had to sell out or close.

In the reach for high living standards and the environment of prosperity, we should be aware that transnational corporations have taken over most of our business world. A transnational corporation with a factory in Asia does not have the same health and safety regulations or the same expenses in wages or environmental regulations as a small business that produces the same goods located across the world from it, perhaps in Australia. Transnational corporations can pack up and move shop whenever required while a small business cannot do this. Transnational corporations also have the ability to control the market price, and thus they are able to destroy small businesses. In such cases, we have big business and governments working together. Such a combination leads to more and more control by government and the power elite (Blasé, 12).

Economic Treaties

Representatives sell us the idea of these economic treaties by claiming they will offer increased competition and a better product with a cheaper price. Americans are so concerned with saving a few dollars that they tend not to think what else may be involved in the economic treaty. Some of the products are in fact cheaper. But is that important enough to overlook any other factors? We may save a few pennies on some products—at least temporarily. But what is the larger cost to small businesses? In effect, small businesses are in trouble, unemployment grows (because the jobs have been transferred out of the country), and a power hierarchy has been set up. Can all of this be happening by accident? Is there some plan to change our economic systems? International financiers and the owners of transnational corporations amass more and more political power and wealth. Have we stopped to think what the end result of this might be?

Privatization

Privatization is another one of those nice-sounding concepts. Under privatization a nation sells off its publicly owned assets and services. The result is that the control of these assets and services end up in the hands of internationalists. This is happening now in Australia, and the Australians will soon be tenants in their own country (Blasé, 12).

What we are witnessing is the greatest transfer of wealth ever undertaken in the history of the world. The wealth is not being transferred among the common people but into the hands of the power elite (Blasé, 12). If we are indeed giving up our wealth, and our claim to more wealth some day, do we really know who is getting the wealth? And do we know who will have the power that accompanies that wealth?

Unskilled Workers

There is also another subtle method of gaining economic advantage. Society has slowly been de-skilled in the workplace in recent years. Mechanics no longer fix problems so much as replace the problems. Panel beaters no longer beat panels, but instead they just replace a plastic piece. Technological progress will bring about some change, of course, but the extent of what has happened goes far beyond simple technological progress. For example, many car parts now come as complete units enclosed in boxes. If a small part breaks down, the whole unit is replaced. The whole unit is more expensive than individual parts might be. But the price is not the main concern of the automotive industry. Primarily, there is less skill in loosening a few screws and fitting in a unit than fixing the unit and the parts themselves. To fix the unit is cheaper and causes less waste. However, it is simpler to prefabricate a unit and replace the whole thing, and it takes a lot less training of mechanics. In this decreasing number of skilled positions, and of workers' abilities, a whole new society is being created where people are more dependent on the system than ever. Thus people will not be able to live on their own, by their own means. As a result, they will depend on the infrastructure of society and the state.

Small Farms Replaced

Notice that small farming has been replaced by large scale farming operations. In fact many farmers are paid not to produce crops. Most farmers are in deep debt because of the rising interest rates and also because of the loss of business due to the government pursuing economic rationalism. Such changes open the way for more and more control by government (Blasé, 15). Results? What are the results of these attempts to control the economics of our country?

Many people have already been lured into dependence on the state. Such dependence occurs through welfare programs, such as the single mother allowance. These benefits are quite easy to obtain, and they actually encourage more people to accept the government as their provider. Notice the recent outcry that "government" (the state or the federal) should be responsible for every citizen getting health insurance. How long has it been the government's responsibility to provide food and clothing and heat and health insurance for the general public? Do you see the trend developing? The more one depends on the state, the more one has to follow the state's rules.

Originally the government was created to defend and protect. Now, though, our government is being asked to provide. Today, many Americans think the government must be the answer to all societal problems. And as the problems grow, so must the government (Fraser and Beeston, 28).

When someone in the community is in need of help, perhaps the help should come from the community. In times past, the community took care of its own people. If someone had a fire or a crop failure or an illness, the whole community gave and supported the need. Such needs should not be passed on to the big political overseers or even to the power elite that contribute nothing to each person's welfare. Because so many people no longer want to be held accountable for their own actions and don't want to get involved with others, they are very susceptible to the deception of socialistic care by the government.

The World Army

While the world is controlled by the economics of banks, and while survival depends on lending money at interest, there will always be the rulers and the ruled. And there will always be a need for war. There will always be vastly more money in circulation than there is actual wealth to back it up. When the borrowers run out of money to pay their lenders, they have two choices: to become enslaved to their debtors, or to conquer their debtors.

In November 1989, U.S. loans to Iraq were guaranteed, providing the money was used to buy U.S. farm produce. Instead, as expected, Saddam Hussein used the money for arms and defaulted on the loans. The U.S. taxpayer picked up the bill for rearming the "enemy." The U.S. funding was done through the Atlantan branch of the Italian government bank, Banco Nazionale del Lavaro (BNL), which loaned $5 billion. Loans from the BNL to Iraq for arms purchases were organized as early as 1984 (Fraser and Beeston).

According to Faser and Beeston, the need for a world army is being presented partly for the reason of planetary security against aggressive extraterrestrials. But mainly it is being presented as the answer to world wars. If people become fearful enough, they will agree to whatever it takes to protect them from terrorism or invasion.

A world army will be achieved through the manipulation of conflicts, leading to extra military powers for the United Nations Peacekeeping Forces. NATO is expanding to absorb more countries of the Eastern Bloc and operates outside of its designated areas. These will fuse to form a world army to enforce the New World Order (Fraser and Beeston).

The framework for the United Nations International Criminal Court was passed in June 1998. The framework will allow the United Nations to detain anyone from any nation and to bring that person before a panel of judges who will hear the case and pass judgment. The crimes that this International Court will deal with are currently "crimes against humanity" and other "enumerated crimes." These courts will have no juries, and there is no appeal process. Because it is an international court, a person's own government will have signed the authority over to the court and can no longer protect that person on trial.

Population Control

Eugenics, which is the control of human reproduction in order to reduce the number of inferior beings, is the main tool of those who want to create a "master race" with desirable genetic characteristics. Eugenics had its highest public profile in Nazi Germany, but it did not stop then. Its use has since continued, but in different ways (Fraser and Beeston). Experiments are ongoing. Birth control is the most current target.

Eugenics policies are funded by the World Bank, which pledged to double the money available for population control. Birth control is now being forced on many developing countries through fear of economic sanctions.

Engineered Wars

War is one of the most effective ways of culling an undesirable population. Thomas Ferguson, a member of the Office of Population Affairs, explains that "to reduce the population quickly, you have to pull all the males into the fighting and kill significant numbers of fertile, child-bearing age females" (Blasé 27).

Indonesia is an example of conflict creation for the purposes of eugenics and corporate control. General Suharto took control of Indonesia in 1965, and since then he has been responsible for 500,000 murders in his own country. This tragedy goes unchallenged in the media. In December of 1975, Indonesia invaded the Portuguese colony of East Timor, and in the following years it proceeded to slaughter 200,000 people, one-third of the Timorese population. The reason? Oil and gas reserves had been discovered off the coast of East Timor, and the multinational oil companies could exploit them only by putting in a corporate-friendly culture (Fraser and Beeston). War is a handy tool to gain control or power over desired people and countries.

31

The Religion of Globalization

Those who are power hungry support cults that promote a world government and believe in the New World Order. These cults include the Moonies, the Church of Scientology, the New Age Movement and others. The reactionary "cult buster" groups, like the Cult Awareness Network set up by Dr. West, is heavily involved in Nazi-style mind control experiments (Fraser and Beeston).

The coming New World Order is based on the occult philosophy known as the "Pure Luciferian Doctrine" or "Illuminism" (Blasé, 18). The World Order entails the process of illumination of the human soul to the state termed "apotheosis." This is the philosophical teaching of the platonic ideal whereby humanity is a singular organism, and it is the chief belief system of Illuminism (Blasé, 16). People who believe this see humanity as a collective being.

Illuminism teaches that mankind collectively is the mind of god. Man is thus god. The individual is merely an illusory part of the whole and thus needs to make sacrifices for thebenefit of this whole. Once we understand this philosophy, we will be able to understand why those who believe it can murder millions of people and see such murder as acceptable, perhaps even desirable. Illuminism teaches that the end justifies the means (Blasé, 16). Many of occult and humanistic beliefs fit beautifully into such doctrine. Because such beliefs seem innocent and non-threatening, it is easy for their adherents to lead followers into the New World System of belief.

The Education Establishment

The way history and science are taught in the schools has been of great importance to our country and to indoctrination into the New World Order. The curriculum is controlled with standardized textbooks, which teachers have to teach from in order to retain their jobs.

Typical lessons taught in today's schools include these (Fraser and Beeston):

1. confusion (there is no meaning),
2. hierarchical position (envy those above, despise those below),
3. dependency (success is measured by the opinion of others; only experts know the truth),
4. obedience (do as others tell you if you want to progress),
5. conformity—the most important of all (do as you are taught to do).

The educational system is responsible for the shaping of most people's worldviews. We all go through school, and, as we do, we are presented with an accepted worldview. An alternative worldview is a threat to the educational system, because it puts into question the administrators' and teachers' roles as authorities. For students to be open minded and willing to challenge what others believe can create much discomfort among teachers and administrators. Students are often taught what to think rather than how to think.

Critical thinking, though it is not taught very often, is a process of thinking that most people should undertake when presented with information. They should take the information and think about it in many ways before accepting it as fact. Critical thinking is basically a learned response—the action of questioning information instead of blindly accepting information (Blaze, 6).

The Media

The media—newspapers, TV, radio and the Internet—provide the exclusive interpretation of information about current affairs. Newspapers are represented as being independent or having a known political leaning. TV is supposedly unbiased and independent. These representations are simply not the case. Information about events comes from "official sources," which can present the view that the power elite wants everyone to accept. Alternatively, news stories are derived from central news agencies (e.g., Reuters), which give everybody the same story (Fraser and Beeston).

The media play into the hands of those who need to create crises to bring people's views into line. For example, four years ago, when the media across America focused almost all attention on butterfly-ballots and elderly voters who could not complete a ballot, the media helped create a constitutional "crisis." As a result, many people are open to having the Constitution amended (Fraser and Beeston, 29). Such emphasis on minor parts of the news allows the media to have great power in influencing and changing people's opinions.

Running a newspaper or a TV station is expensive, which limits the organizations that can operate one. The big businesses that do own and operate such media are obviously financially successful in the System. Consequently, they have an interest in maintaining the status quo so that they can continue to profit and be successful. Opinions and stories that challenge the establishment are therefore of no interest to these companies.

In addition, the media industry is advertising-based, with prices of newspapers kept below the manufacturing costs by advertising income (Fraser and Beeston). The threat of withdrawing advertising is generally sufficient to ensure that the media owners will filter the stories they present. If one unacceptable story or news item slips through, business organizations often combine forces to pressure editors into reviewing their content. They create such pressure through letters, lawsuits and even parliamentary bills. One example of these so-called "flack machines" is Accuracy in Media (AIM), a collection of corporate giants, which includes eight oil companies, whose function is to maintain a corporate-friendly media in the U.S.

CHAPTER 4:
ONE WORLD GOVERNMENT

"Crisis" is the key word in establishing a New World Order or a One World Government. To help complacent Americans accept the new government intrusions, President Clinton's propagandists instilled fear of just about every crisis they could think of. The buzzword of the nineties was "crisis." We were told we had a healthcare "crisis"—justifying the government takeover of one-seventh of the U.S. economy. We were told we had an ecological "crisis"—justifying the government's imposition of far-reaching new regulations on businesses. We were told we had a childcare "crisis"—justifying the government extending its reach into family care (Fraser and Beeston, 29). The Clinton administration went a long way in obtaining a federal takeover of the management of American business, healthcare, education and the American family (Fraser and Beeston, 28).

Most Americans believe it is impossible to bring a totalitarian socialist world government into the United States because the people would never agree to it. However, Blasé asks, would it be possible to bring one in without the people realizing it? There are two critical areas that would allow such a change in government. First, mind control. Second, the monetary system. Manipulation in both of those areas would bring us into the one world government system (Blasé 4, 5), and most people would not even be aware it was happening.

CHAPTER 5:
MIND CONTROL

Mind control experiments have been going on for decades, using esoteric knowledge about the human psyche.

Mass hypnosis is possible by the repetition of a basic theme until it is accepted as fact by the subconscious and then the conscious mind. Such messages can be flashed during TV programs and films and are not perceived by the eyes and conscious minds. The mesmerizing and sedating effect of television puts the subconscious mind into an ideal state to receive messages sent to the psyche via carrier TV/radio waves. Technology already exists whereby thoughts can be induced by stimulating brainwaves (Fraser and Beeston).

Mind Control Techniques

Mind control is merely the influence and control of what we think and of the way we think. There are many ways to accomplish such influence over our thinking, even if it does not fully control our minds.

1. **Limited Information.** The main method of mind control is the control of the information Americans receive. By limiting the information available, the media also limit the thoughts that people think.
2. **Distracted Thinking.** People are also kept occupied—busy with side issues of little importance.

If the people get engrossed in minor issues, they will leave the major issues alone.

3. **Confusion.** Confused meanings of words, or multiple meanings of words, also keep people from understanding the full significance of what is going on. For example, there is much debate over the meaning of the word "democracy." In what way is the United States a democracy, and in what way is it instead a republic?

4. **Side Issues Made Major.** Politicians always like to talk about debt and taxes. They know that people will vote for the candidate that will cost them less. People are so worried about money that they forget other issues, such as "freedom" and "liberty."

5. **Prejudicial Slants.** The news media put a slant on news stories to condition people how to think. Also, other TV programs are used to condition people to see the world in new ways—the ways depicted in the films and sitcoms. People are so suggestible that such a ploy is not difficult. They may be horrified at the ideas at first, but when new ideas are accompanied with comedy, it will not be long before those ideas are accepted.

6. **A Few Major Owners.** A few corporations own most media, and the slant presented must fall in line with the corporation policies. Next time you watch the news, change stations and you will notice that every station has the same headlines and the same slant or viewpoint on each story. Many events occur in the world every day—why the same ones reported on every network? If there were real competition, there would be differences in the stories and the slants.

7. **Hypnotic Lack of Thinking.** The TV screen induces a mild hypnotic state that impairs the viewer's critical thinking. Many commercials have flashing

lights and lots of quick movement to add to the hypnotic trance. In this state, the mind is more suggestible and liable to mental programming. Simply observing someone watching TV will give you an example of this altered state of mind.

8. Attention Spans. Short news bulletins and commercials have conditioned people to have short attention spans. As a result of the short attention spans, people do not usually delve deeply into topics of concern.

Mind control, then, is not the major, life-changing, super-surgical event we see in science fiction movies. True, there is a physical mind control—through the use of drugs, electromagnetic waves and neuro-implants—to accomplish major changes in thinking. However, most mind control is nothing like those major events. Instead, it is an everyday subtle guiding of the mind to work in certain ways. The mind is being programmed without the person being aware of the programming.

Subliminal Suggestion

One form of mind control was used for commercial benefits—products were sold through subliminal suggestion. Thirty to forty years ago, experiments, took place using TV and movie screens. Each frame of a video or film goes by so quickly that one frame is indecipherable by the human eye. So testers inserted one frame at a time of a particular product to those watching without the viewers ever being aware of seeing the product. For example, one frame of a TV program would show a picture of a product, such as potato chips. The test was to find out how many of those people who had seen the picture of potato chips would actually buy them. The testers discovered that, the day after showing the one frame of potato chips, the purchase of potato chips increased 50 percent over the usual day's purchases.

Movie theaters tried it with popcorn and cokes. Slipping a one-frame picture of popcorn or a coke into the film every ten minutes or so put the idea in the minds of viewers without them ever being aware of it. The power of suggestion was so strong that sales of popcorn and coke increased 65 percent over the movies with no subliminal suggestion frames in the films. Those people who had a sudden urge to go to the lobby and buy popcorn had no idea why they felt the urge to do so. We know, though, that they had been programmed to do so through subliminal suggestion, a very powerful form of mind control.

This kind of mind control is subtle and works subconsciously at the level of suggestion. Subliminal experiments have been proved effective in many areas, especially in selling products, establishing needs and affecting opinions. (People who did not realize they had a position on an issue discovered that they had strong opinions—those presented to them subliminally in a movie or on TV). Such practices are now illegal. We should be able to believe that they are no longer in use—for any reason. However, since we cannot see the suggestion in the movie or video, how can we be sure?

This subliminal form of mind control seems rather non-threatening. However, if such technology can be used for unimportant things such as selling products, it can also be used for more significant things, such as programming one's thinking. Also, there are much more serious methods of controlling what one thinks.

Extreme Control

The most sinister and far-reaching mind control program is Project MK Ultra, run on behalf of the CIA. During Operation Paperclip, Nazi scientists were moved to the U.S. and given prestigious positions at the leading colleges and Universities and NASA after World War II. Their goal was to continue their experiments on thousands of "lesser human beings"—prisoners, mental patients, victims of pedophilia, etc. Experiments have included removing a person's existing personality by electrotherapy and then programming a new one by psychic driving. This change makes the "subject" obsessed with certain ideas and is undoubtedly the way to program so-called lone assassins (Fraser and Beeston).

A Microchipped Population
The ideal form of control will be via a microchipped population connected to a global computer. Money will become obsolete, and all financial transactions will be via a microchip inserted under the skin, used in much the same way as a credit or smart card. Swipe your wrist over the sensor to pay for your goods. It is convenient and easy. It enables the power elite people to have complete knowledge about every person and every transaction. If your wrist is refused for some reason, you will be prevented from buying anything (Fraser and Beeston).

In 1994, the Intel Corporation was given a five-year contract to research an under-the-skin microchip for identity/financial transactions. Moves to implement this plan of payment are already underway, and public opinion is being softened up to accept it. It is already being used for some purposes: to find pets if they wander away), to tag newborn babies in maternity wards and to tag criminals electronically. A need for identity cards is being presented as a way of combating crime. Supermarkets are experimenting with bar-coded cards to keep a tally of purchases without the need for a checkout assistant. The pay-at-the-pump system, a form of microchipped information, is in wide use at most gas stations (Fraser and Beeston).

IBM has already developed an invisible bar coding

system of three sets of six numbers that is painless and can be installed on the skin by laser in a fraction of a second. It is currently being used on cattle, and it can be "installed" without the person even being aware of its existence.

Dr. Carl W. Sanders is an electronics engineer, inventor, author and consultant with various government organizations, as well as with IBM and General Electric. He spent thirty-two years developing microchip technology for use in medicine. He came up with a tiny chip that is recharged by body temperature, whose prime location would be in the forehead (just below the hairline) or on the back of the hand. The chip he developed would contain details of a person's name, a picture of the face, a security number, a fingerprint, a physical description, family history, an address and occupation, income tax information and any criminal record. The chip has been tested as a contraception device in India and as a behavior modifier in Vietnam veterans. Bills have been put before Congress in the USA to allow the government to microchip children at birth (Fraser and Beeston).

Not only can the chip send messages to a computer, messages can also be sent the other way—from the computer to the person wearing the chip. These messages are sent via satellite TV receivers, which can be programmed through remote control.

In 1975, a man named Dannion Brinkley was struck by lightning and had a near death experience, which he recounts in his book, *Saved by the Light.* During the twenty-eight minutes he was officially dead, a spirit being led him through a dark tunnel to a crystal city. He recalls a total of 117 events shown to him on a screen pertaining to predicted events on Earth between 1975 and 2000. At the time the book was released in 1994, ninety-five of these events had occurred. One of the final visions he received was of a computer chip technology slowly infiltrating every aspect of our day-to-day lives. Eventually a computer chip would be inserted under the skin of every member of the Earth's population containing the total information of everyone's medical history, social status, and credit rating. Those who refused chips would be unemployable (Fraser and Beeston).

CHAPTER 6:
CONCLUSION

In order to bring about a New World Order, the Old World Order had to be destroyed. The Old World Order was built on a Judeo-Christian foundation. This foundation proved very successful. Compare the nations on earth that were built on the Judeo-Christian foundation to those nations been built on a pagan foundation. The Judeo-Christian nations have had freedom, liberty and opportunity for all who lived there whether they believed in those concepts or not.

In the nations built on a Judeo-Christian foundation, the people are declared sovereigns with unalienable rights granted by God. The government has the task of protecting these rights. A higher authority than men grants the right to freedom, liberty and property, and thus men cannot overrule this authority. This is the foundation that the United States was built on.

On the other end of the spectrum, take a look at the United Nations Charter and other related documents. You will clearly see that individual rights are a privilege and are granted by the government. A big difference! If the people's individual rights are granted by the government, then the government can take those rights away (Blasé, 15).

Mass manipulation and mind control techniques have been used on the people of the world to wear away the foundation of the Judeo-Christian heritage our country is based on. Humanists, those practicing the occult, atheists and others have passed legislation, and have used media, religion and education to slowly break down the old way of doing things. As the old is broken down, we come closer and closer to a world government.

BIBLIOGRAPHY
AND FURTHER READING

Adelmann, Bo. 1986. "The Federal Reserve System." *The New American*, October 17.

Blasé, William. "It's Time to Awaken from Sleep!" wblase@zmnet.com. or Courier@zianet.com.

Charter of the United Nations; various other United Nations documents and related documents.

Constantine, Alex. 1997. *CIA Mind Control Operations in America*. Port Townsend, WA: Feral House.

Declaration of a Global Ethic. 1993. Parliament of World Religions under the United Nations.

The Fed: Our Central Bank. Publication by the Federal Reserve Bank of Chicago.

Flaherty, Edward, Ph.D. Website refuting the Conspiracy Theory. http://www.cofc.edu/~flaherty/index.html.

Fraser, Ivan, and Mark Beeston. "The Brotherhood and the Manipulation of Society." 44 pages. http://www.mysteries-megasite.com/main/bigsearch/newworldorder.html.

Golitsyn, Anatoly. 1984. *New Lies for Old.* New York: Dodd, Mead, and Co.

Grenville, J. 1994. *A Collins History of the World in the Twentieth Century.* New York: HarperCollins.

Gurudus. 1996. *Treason: The New World Order.* Boulder, CO: Cassandra Press

Hermann, Robert A. 1994. *Your Endangered Mind.* http://www.raherrmann.com/gsc.htm

Hoar, William P. *Architects of Conspiracy.* 1984. Belmont, MA: Western Islands.

Jacobson, Steven. 1991. *Mind Control in America* (audiotape). MCIA Media.

Jasper, William. 1992. *Global Tyranny: Step by step.* Belmont, MA: Western Islands.

Johansen, Robert C. 1980. "Models of World Order," in *Dilemmas of War and Peace.* http://therearenosunglasses.wordpress.com/2008/11/06/dilemmas-of-war-and-peace-new-world-order/

Kah, Gary H. 1992. *En Route to Global Occupation.* Fayetteville, LA: Huntington House Publishers.

Kjos, Berit. 1995. *Brave New Schools.* Eugene, OR: Harvest House Publishers.

Our Global Neighborhood. 1993. Commission on Global Governance,

Robertson, Pat. 1991. *The New World Order*. Dallas: Word Publishing.

Strachan, Graham. 1997. *Economic Rationalism: A Disaster for Australia*. Kalgoorlie, Australia: Kalgoorlie Press.

Wardner, James W., Dr. 1993. *The Planned Destruction of America*. Orlando, FL: Longwood Communications.

ONE FINAL WORD

America as we know her will cease to exist unless Americans stop the current trends.

America is in peril. Various forces seek to destroy what her Founding Fathers established by the grace of God.

The United States of America was founded as a Christian nation, for that is what the vast majority of Americans were. I believe the majority of Americans still are Christians. A nation is what its people are.

America was intended to be a Holy Land, divinely set apart by God as a light shining on a hill. Right now, America is in shackles and her freedom is in jeopardy. A people may never secure its freedom once and for all time; it must be ready to forever pay the price to preserve its freedom until the Almighty restores the lost paradise.

Americans obviously have tough decisions to make.

PROPHETIC WARNINGS
TO AMERICA

"If men, through fear, fraud, or mistake, should in terms renounce or give up any natural right, the eternal law of reason and the grand end of society would absolutely vacate such renunciation. The right to freedom being the gift of god, it is not in the power of man to alienate this gift and voluntarily become a slave."

—Samuel Adams
The Father of the American Revolution

"We do not have a government armed with suffered power to tame the animal passions of mankind. The Constitution is made only for a moral and a religious people. It is wholly inadequate for the government of any other."

—President John Adams

"If ever time should come, when vain and aspiring men shall possess the highest seats in Government, our country will stand in need of its experienced patriots to prevent its ruin."

—Samuel Adams

"Among the natural rights of the Colonists are these: First, a right to life; Secondly, to liberty; Thirdly, to property; together with the right to support and defend them in the best manner they can."

—Samuel Adams
"Rights of the Colonists," November 1772

"You need only reflect that one of the best ways to get yourself a reputation as a dangerous citizen these days is to go about repeating the very phrases which our founding fathers used in their struggle for independence."

—C. A. Beard

"When they came to Capernaum those who collected tax money came to Peter and said, 'Does your master not pay taxes?' He said, 'Yes.' When he came into the house Jesus stopped him, saying, 'What do you think, Simon? From whom do the kings of the earth take custom or taxes? From their own children, or from strangers?' Peter replied, 'From strangers.' Jesus said, 'Then the children are free' " (*Mt. 17:24–26*).

—The Holy Bible

"Property: Rightful dominion over external objects; ownership; the unrestricted and exclusive right to a thing; Property is the highest right a man can have to anything."

—Black's Law Dictionary, Second Edition, 1891

"Income Tax: A tax on the yearly profits arising from property, professions, trades, and offices."

—Black's Law Dictionary Second Edition, 1891

"Our task of creating a Socialist America can only succeed when those who would resist us have been totally disarmed."

—Sarah Brady

"I do solemnly swear that I will support and defend the Constitution of the United States against all enemies, foreign and domestic; that I will bear true faith and allegiance to the same; that I take this obligation freely, without any mental reservation or purpose of evasion: and that I will well and faithfully discharge the duties of

the office on which I am about to enter. So help me, God."
—Congressional Oath of Office

"As civil rulers, not having their duty to the people duly before them, may attempt to tyrannize, and as the military forces which must be occasionally raised to defend our country, might pervert their power to the injury of their fellow citizens, the people are confirmed by the next article [the Second Amendment] in their right to keep and bear their private arms."
—Trence Coxe under the pseudonym "A Pennsylvanian" From "Remarks on the First Part of the Amendments to the Federal Constitution," Published in the Philadelphia Federal Gazette, 18 June 1789

"Find out just what the people will submit to, and you have found out the exact amount of injustice and wrong which will be imposed upon them; and these will continue until they are resisted with either words or blows, or with both. The limits of tyrants are prescribed by the endurance of those whom they oppress."
—Frederick Douglas (1857)

"The hardest thing in the world to understand is the income tax."
—Albert Einstein

"It is well that the people of the nation do not understand our banking and monetary system, for if they did, I believe there would be a revolution before tomorrow morning"
—Henry Ford

"Those who give up essential liberties for temporary safety deserve neither liberty nor safety."

—*Benjamin Franklin*

"Step by Step the International Financiers and those who represent them gain ownership of real assets as collateral for the debt interest. Now these assets are not directly acquired by the Federal Reserve but the wealth is acquired through the continual process of inflation which is merely the result of the flooding of the economy with fiat money. This system ensures that the wealth is slowly transferred from the middle class to the upper class."

—*Fraser and Beeston*

"What, sir, is the use of a militia? It is to prevent the establishment of a standing army, the bane of liberty... Whenever Governments mean to invade the rights and liberties of the people, they always attempt to destroy the militia, in order to raise an army upon their ruins."

—*Representative Elbridge Gerry, Massachusetts, I Annals of Congress at 750, 8/17/1789*

"The legal right of the taxpayer to decrease the amount of what otherwise would be his taxes or altogether avoid them by means which the law permits, cannot be doubted."

—*Gregory v. Helvering, 293 U.S. 465*

"The great object is that everyman be armed. Everyone who is able may have a gun."

—*Patrick Henry
At the Virginia Convention on the ratification of the Constitution*

"I know not what course others may take, but as for me, give me liberty or give me death."
—*Patrick Henry*

"The best yardstick of the effectiveness of the fight against Communism is the fury of the smear attacks against the fighter."
—*J. Edgar Hoover*

"The democracy will cease to exist when you take away from those who are willing to work and give to those who would not."
—*President Thomas Jefferson*

"To compel a man to subsidize with his taxes the propagation of ideas which he disbelieves and abhors is sinful and tyrannical."
—*President Thomas Jefferson*

"When we get piled upon one another in large cities, as in Europe, we shall become as corrupt as Europe."

—*President Thomas Jefferson*
"Still one thing more, fellow citizens, a wise and frugal government which shall restrain men from injuring one another, shall leave them otherwise free to regulate their own pursuits of industry and improvement, and shall not take from the mouth of labor the bread it has earned. This is the sum of good government."
—*President Thomas Jefferson, First Inaugural Address*

"I predict future happiness for Americans if they can prevent the government from wasting the labors of the people under the pretense of taking care of them."
—*President Thomas Jefferson*

"Fear can only prevail when victims are ignorant of the facts."

—President Thomas Jefferson

"The strongest reason for the people to retain the right to keep and bear arms is, as a last resort, to protect themselves against tyranny in government."

—President Thomas Jefferson

"No free man shall ever be debarred the use of arms."

—President Thomas Jefferson

"Peace, commerce, and honest friendship with all nations, entangling alliances with none."

—President Thomas Jefferson, First Inaugural Address

"A government that is large enough to supply everything you need is large enough to take everything you have."

—President Thomas Jefferson

"I sincerely believe that banking institutions are more dangerous to our liberties than standing armies. If the American people ever allow private banks to control the issue of their currency, first by inflation, then by deflation, the banks and corporations that will grow up around the banks will deprive the people of all property until their children wake up homeless on the continent their fathers conquered."

—President Thomas Jefferson

"The tree of liberty must be watered periodically with the blood of tyrants and patriots alike. It is its natural manure."

—President Thomas Jefferson

"A strong body makes the mind strong. As to the species of exercises, I advise the gun. While this gives moderate exercise to the body, it gives boldness, enterprise and independence to the mind. Games played with the ball and others of that nature, are too violent for the body and stamp no character on the mind. Let your gun therefore be the constant companion of your walks."
—President Thomas Jefferson

"The high office of President has been used to foment a plot to destroy the American's freedom, and before I leave office I must inform the citizen of his plight."
—President John F. Kennedy
At Columbia University, ten days before his assassination

"We shall cause the United States to spend itself to destruction."
—Lenin

"This nation can never be conquered from without. If it is ever to fall it will be from within."
—President Abraham Lincoln

"As usurpation is the exercise of power, which another hath a right to; so tyranny is the exercise of power beyond right, which nobody can have a right to."
—John Locke, "Of Civil Government," 1689

"I believe there are more instances of the abridgment of freedom of the people by gradual and silent encroachment of those in power than by violent and sudden usurpations."
—President James Madison

"The Federal Reserve Bank is 'a super-state' controlled by international bankers and international industrialists acting together to enslave the world for their own pleasure."

—Former Congressman Louis McFadden
Former Chairman, House Committee on Banking and
Currency

"We have in this country one of the most corrupt institutions the world has ever known. I refer to the Federal Reserve Board and the Federal Reserve Banks...They are, not government institutions. They are private monopolies which prey upon the people of these United States for the benefit of themselves and their foreign customers..."

—Senator Louis T. McFadden
Chairman of the U.S. Banking & Currency Commission

"Those that create and issue the money and credit direct the policies of government and hold in their hands the destiny of the people."

—Reginald McKenna
Former President of the Midlands Bank of England

"In the United States today we have in effect two governments. We have the duly constituted government. Then we have an independent, uncontrolled and uncoordinated government in the Federal Reserve System, operating the money powers reserved to Congress by the Constitution"

—Congressman Wright Patman
Former Chairman of the House Banking Committee

"Patriotism means to stand by the country. It does not mean to stand by the President or any other public office save exactly to the degree in which he himself stands by the country."

—President Theodore Roosevelt

"No one is bound to obey an unconstitutional law and no courts are bound to enforce it."

—Sixteenth American Jurisprudence
Second Edition, Section 177

"The highest level of prosperity occurs when there is a free-market economy and a minimum of government regulations."

—Adam Smith, "The Wealth of Nations"

"'Income,' as used in the statute should be given the meaning so as not to include everything that comes in. The true function of the words 'gain' and 'profit' is to limit the meaning of the word income."

—So. Pacific v. Lower, 238 F 847

"All socialism involves slavery."

—Herbert Spencer

"All government without the consent of the governed is the very definition of slavery."

—Jonathan Swift

"The tax power has been used by the national government as a weapon to take over, one by one, subjects traditionally within the orbit of state police power."

—Chief Justice Taft

"All laws which are repugnant to the Constitution are null and void."

—U.S. Supreme Court
Marbury v. Madison, 2Cranch 5 U.S. (1803)

"None are more hopelessly enslaved than those who falsely believe they are free."

—Johann W. Von Goethe

"It is impossible to rightly govern the world without God or the Bible." And "Reason and experience forbid us to expect public morality in the absence of religious principle."

—President George Washington

"Government is not reason; it is not eloquence; it is force! Like fire, it is a dangerous servant and a fearful master."

—President George Washington

"God grants liberty only to those who love it, and are always ready to guard and defend it."

—Daniel Webster

"An Unconstitutional Act is not a law; it confers no rights; it imposes no duties; it affords no protection; it creates no office; it is, in legal contemplation, as inoperative as though it had never been passed."

—U.S. Supreme Court Norton V. Shelby County,
118 U.S. 425, 442

"If we abide by the principles taught in the Bible, our nation will go on prospering."

—Daniel Webster

"God grants liberty only to those who love it, and are always ready to guard and defend it."

—Daniel Webster

"One of the main purposes for the control and power of the Establishment media is to keep the masses deceived and ignorant about their rights and oppressions of their rights."

—Charles Weisman

COMMUNIST RULES
FOR REVOLUTION

Captured by the Allies in Dusseldorf, Germany
1919

A. Corrupt the young, get them away from religion. Get them interested in sex. Make them superficial, destroy their ruggedness.

B. Get control of all means of publicity and thereby:
  1. Get people's mind off their government by focusing their attention on athletics, sexy books, and plays and other trivialities.
  2. Divide the people into hostile groups by constantly harping on controversial matters of no importance.
  3. Destroy the people's faith in their natural leaders by holding the latter up to contempt, ridicule, and obloquy.
  4. Always preach true democracy but seize power as fast and as ruthlessly as possible.
  5. By encouraging government extravagance, destroy its credit, produce fear of inflation with rising prices and general discontent.
  6. Foment unnecessary strikes in vital industries, encourage civil disorders, and foster a lenient and soft attitude on the part of government toward such disorders.
  7. By specious argument cause the breakdown of the old moral virtues: honesty, sobriety, continence, faith in the pledged word, ruggedness.

C. Cause the registration of all firearms on some pretext, with a view of confiscating them and leaving the population helpless.

THE COMMUNIST TAKEOVER OF AMERICA

45 Declared Goals

Communist Goals (1963) Congressional Record-- Appendix, pp. A34-A35 January 10, 1963

Current Communist Goals EXTENSION OF REMARKS OF HON. A. S. HERLONG, JR. OF FLORIDA IN THE HOUSE OF REPRESENTATIVES Thursday, January 10, 1963 .

Mr. HERLONG. Mr. Speaker, Mrs. Patricia Nordman of De Land, Fla., is an ardent and articulate opponent of communism, and until recently published the *De Land Courier*, which she dedicated to the purpose of alerting the public to the dangers of communism in America.

At Mrs. Nordman's request, I include in the RECORD, under unanimous consent, the following "Current Communist Goals," which she identifies as an excerpt from "The Naked Communist," by Cleon Skousen:

[From "The Naked Communist," by Cleon Skousen]

1. U.S. acceptance of coexistence as the only alternative to atomic war.
2. U.S. willingness to capitulate in preference to engaging in atomic war.

3. Develop the illusion that total disarmament [by] the United States would be a demonstration of moral strength.

4. Permit free trade between all nations regardless of Communist affiliation and regardless of whether or not items could be used for war.

5. Extension of long-term loans to Russia and Soviet satellites.

6. Provide American aid to all nations regardless of Communist domination.

7. Grant recognition of Red China. Admission of Red China to the U.N.

8. Set up East and West Germany as separate states in spite of Khrushchev's promise in 1955 to settle the German question by free elections under supervision of the U.N.

9. Prolong the conferences to ban atomic tests because the United States has agreed to suspend tests as long as negotiations are in progress.

10. Allow all Soviet satellites individual representation in the U.N.

11. Promote the U.N. as the only hope for mankind. If its charter is rewritten, demand that it be set up as a one-world government with its own independent armed forces. (Some Communist leaders believe the world can be taken over as easily by the U.N. as by Moscow. Sometimes these two centers compete with each other as they are now doing in the Congo.)

12. Resist any attempt to outlaw the Communist Party.

13. Do away with all loyalty oaths.

14. Continue giving Russia access to the U.S. Patent Office.

15. Capture one or both of the political parties in the United States.

16. Use technical decisions of the courts to weaken

basic American institutions by claiming their activities violate civil rights.

17. Get control of the schools. Use them as transmission belts for socialism and current Communist propaganda. Soften the curriculum. Get control of teachers' associations. Put the party line in textbooks.

18. Gain control of all student newspapers.

19. Use student riots to foment public protests against programs or organizations which are under Communist attack.

20. Infiltrate the press. Get control of book-review assignments, editorial writing, policy-making positions.

21. Gain control of key positions in radio, TV, and motion pictures.

22. Continue discrediting American culture by degrading all forms of artistic expression. An American Communist cell was told to "eliminate all good sculpture from parks and buildings, substitute shapeless, awkward and meaningless forms."

23. Control art critics and directors of art museums. "Our plan is to promote ugliness, repulsive, meaningless art."

24. Eliminate all laws governing obscenity by calling them "censorship" and a violation of free speech and free press.

25. Break down cultural standards of morality by promoting pornography and obscenity in books, magazines, motion pictures, radio, and TV.

26. Present homosexuality, degeneracy and promiscuity as "normal, natural, healthy."

27. Infiltrate the churches and replace revealed religion with "social" religion. Discredit the Bible and emphasize the need for intellectual maturity, which does not need a "religious crutch."

28. Eliminate prayer or any phase of religious expression in the schools on the ground that it violates the principle of "separation of church and state."
29. Discredit the American Constitution by calling it inadequate, old-fashioned, out of step with modern needs, a hindrance to cooperation between nations on a worldwide basis.
30. Discredit the American Founding Fathers. Present them as selfish aristocrats who had no concern for the "common man."
31. Belittle all forms of American culture and discourage the teaching of American history on the ground that it was only a minor part of the "big picture." Give more emphasis to Russian history since the Communists took over.
32. Support any socialist movement to give centralized control over any part of the culture—education, social agencies, welfare programs, mental health clinics, etc.
33. Eliminate all laws or procedures which interfere with the operation of the Communist apparatus.
34. Eliminate the House Committee on Un-American Activities.
35. Discredit and eventually dismantle the FBI.
36. Infiltrate and gain control of more unions.
37. Infiltrate and gain control of big business.
38. Transfer some of the powers of arrest from the police to social agencies. Treat all behavioral problems as psychiatric disorders which no one but psychiatrists can understand [or treat].
39. Dominate the psychiatric profession and use mental health laws as a means of gaining coercive control over those who oppose Communist goals.
40. Discredit the family as an institution. Encourage promiscuity and easy divorce.

41. Emphasize the need to raise children away from the negative influence of parents. Attribute prejudices, mental blocks and retarding of children to suppressive influence of parents.

42. Create the impression that violence and insurrection are legitimate aspects of the American tradition; that students and special-interest groups should rise up and use ["]united force ["] to solve economic, political or social problems.

43. Overthrow all colonial governments before native populations are ready for self-government.

44. Internationalize the Panama Canal.

45. Repeal the Connally reservation so the United States cannot prevent the World Court from seizing jurisdiction [over domestic problems. Give the World Court jurisdiction] over nations and individuals alike.

Sources are listed below.

Microfilm: California State University at San Jose Clark Library, Government Floor Phone (408) 924-2770 Microfilm Call Number: J 11.R5

Congressional Record, Vol. 109 88th Congress, 1st Session Appendix Pages A1–A2842 Jan. 9-May 7, 1963 Reel 12

KING SOLOMON
REFUTES COMMUNISM

"My son, if sinners entice thee, consent thou not. If they say, Come with us, let us lay wait for blood, let us lurk privily for the innocent without cause: Let us swallow them up alive as the grave; and whole, as those that go down into the pit: We shall find all precious substance, we shall fill our houses with spoil: Cast in thy lot among us; let us all have one purse: My son, walk not thou in the way with them; refrain thy foot from their path: For their feet run to evil, and make haste to shed blood. Surely in vain the net is spread in the sight of any bird. And they lay wait for their *own* blood; they lurk privily for their *own* lives. So *are* the ways of every one that is greedy of gain; *which* taketh away the life of the owners thereof."

—*King Solomon*
Proverbs 1:10-19, KJV

ABOUT THE AUTHOR

CHAPLAIN (MAJOR) JAMES F. LINZEY, ARNG (RET.) is a retired United States Army Chaplain, having served a combined total of nearly twenty-four years of active duty and reserve duty. Jim began his military career in the United States Air Force on November 5, 1985. On January 4, 1998, he left the Air Force to join the Army. Among Jim's assignments were tours of duty at Maxwell Air Force Base, Montgomery, Alabama, where he attended Air University. Among many subjects, he focused his studies on Leadership Awareness, Team Awareness and Team Leadership. Among the Professional Military Education schools and courses he attended were the Air Force Officers' Orientation Course, the Chaplains Officers' Basic Course, the Chaplains Officers' Advanced Course, the Squadron Officers' School, the Combined Arms and Services Staff School, and the Command and General Staff College.

Military assignments over his twenty-four-year career include Command Chaplain, 5035th Garrison Support Unit, Fort Bliss, Texas; Command Chaplain, Cluster III, Operation Noble Eagle II, White Sands Missile Range, New Mexico, under the Department of Homeland

Security; and Chaplain for the Officer Candidate School at Fort Mead, South Dakota. In the course of his career, Jim trained military personnel in principles and practices of character-based leadership in Joint-Military Leadership Training at the Armed Forces Staff College and aboard the USS *Briscoe* at the Naval Air Station, Norfolk, Virginia, and in the Quartermaster's Officers' Basic Course and Non-commissioned Officers seminars at Fort Lee, Virginia. Jim applied his training while serving on the Leadership Panel at the United States Army Cadet Command's Leader's Training Course at Fort Knox, Kentucky, as its first full-time chaplain. Jim retired from the U.S. Army on June 29, 2009 with an Honorable Discharge at the rank of Major.

Jim attended the Billy Graham School of Evangelism in Ashville, North Carolina. He received a Bachelor of Arts degree from Vanguard University of Southern California, Costa Mesa, California; a Master of Divinity degree from Fuller Theological Seminary, Pasadena, California; and a Doctor of Divinity degree from Kingsway Theological Seminary, Des Moines, Iowa.

Other appearances, including media consist of ABC News, CBS News, CNN News, the Christian Broadcasting Network and the *Glenn Beck Show*. He was a guest on Daystar Television Network, God's Learning Channel, SON Broadcasting Network and Trinity Broadcasting Network. Jim hosted his own television series, which aired on various networks around the world. He also served as a missionary and conducted evangelistic crusades. He supports missions projects in Mexico, the Philippines, India and Africa.

Jim is listed in *Who's Who in America, Who's Who in the World*, the *International Centre of Biography in Cambridge, England*, and *2000 Intellectuals of the 21st Century*.